God Took A Day Off

Why Can't I?

God Took A Day Off

Why Can't I?

a Christian life coach's guide to great results with less effort

ANDREA MOORE

Miller.Moore
Publishing

God Took A Day Off, Why Can't I?
by Andrea Moore

Be Your Best Book Series - Sabbath

Copyright © 2011

Cover Design and Book Layout: Love and Change Studios LLC

Edited By: J.R. Wilco

Photos by: Careese Vieregge Photography

Published By: Miller-Moore Publishing

ISBN: 978-0-9840074-1-7

All rights reserved. This book, or parts thereof, may not be reproduced in any form without permission from the publisher; exceptions are made for brief excerpts used in published reviews.

Biblical references are taken from the King James Version,
New King James Version, New American Standard,
the New International Version
and The Message as noted.

Greek and Hebrew meanings courtesy of Blue Letter Bible.

Contact the author at:
www.HisDesignForSuccess.com

This book is available in quantity discounts for bulk purchases.

For further information, please email Info@Hisdesignforsuccess.com
Printed in the United States of America.

To our Heavenly Father: Thank you for scheduling breaks for us to pause and be recharged!

To my amazing husband and our three dynamic little men: Thank you so very much for every prayer and warm hug. You are my inspirations and the smiles I hold in my heart.

To Grandma & PaPa, Granny & PaPa, Gramps & Grammy & our dear WaWa: Thank you for all the love, strength and support. We love you dearly.

To all our friends and family: Your love, prayers and encouragement have been invaluable. Thanks for always believing in us -- and what God has set before us.

Table of Contents

Why I wrote this book

Chapter 1: Good is not always God 7

Chapter 2: Why we need rest 15

Chapter 3: What is a Sabbath? 23

Chapter 4: What a Sabbath looks like 33

Chapter 5: Our birthmark 41

Chapter 6: How I spend my Sabbath 47

Chapter 7: Overcoming obstacles 55

Chapter 8: Faith to rest 65

Chapter 9: Not a demand, but a delight 73

Chapter 10: Preparing and protecting 81

Chapter 11: Freedom 87

Acknowledgments 91

References 92

Additional Life Balance Wheels 95

Why I wrote this book

Have you ever wanted to rest or slow down, but knew you couldn't because you had too much going on?

Have you ever felt guilty for sitting down, or found yourself uncomfortable just being still?

If so, I can definitely relate. I used to regularly finish one task, only to turn around and find there were half a dozen chores screaming for my attention.

I wrote this book because so many people asked me how I was able to take a Sabbath and still remain productive. Many were also curious as to what a day of rest involved. So I studied and set out to present a clear picture of what a Sabbath is and how anyone can take one and reap the benefits.

The tools the world gives us to deal with the pressures we live under are merely band-aids. They manage the symptoms, but they fail to create any lasting change. A new approach is needed, or in this case, a much older one.

In the following chapters, we will discuss what we're missing when we don't allow ourselves to rest. We will discover the benefits of a day of rest and how we really can fit one into an already hectic life.

What happened to me

As the co-captain of the University of Alabama's Crimson Tide volleyball team, I placed a high value on always trying to set a great example. I rested very little while working to attain my personal goals. Upon graduating with a degree in Communications, I surrendered my life over to what the Lord had for me and began to build a relationship with Him.

Slowly, I came to realize that my desire to enter the ministry full-time outweighed every other dream, including that of a career in television. I threw myself into the ministry but found that instead of spending quality time with Him, I focused on the things I could do for His glory.

After a few years, the work I had once been so thrilled to take part in had become a burden. My pursuit to accomplish every single task pushed my life out of balance.

In the midst of this struggle, I heard one of my mentors, Mrs. Helen Hall, discuss the Sabbath and its value for our lives today. I knew God wanted me to learn to rest in Him, but I did not join my faith with the message to make it a lifestyle. My time in ministry was filled with great experiences and interesting adventures, but my endless to-do list had me completely burned out.

Why you should read this

Without realizing it, most of us trust more in what we can achieve for God than in what He can do through us. I've heard people

Why I wrote this book

say, "I know that I should rest, but I can't when there's still so much to do!"

As a life coach, I have had several clients come to me feeling frustrated and worn out, with a lack of clarity regarding personal direction. Together we have faced many of the things I will discuss within the following pages.

A need for more rest might not have been an idea that you would have come up with on your own. Instead, this book may be the Lord's way of prompting you to prepare yourself for what He's wanting to do in your life.

In the pages that follow, we are going to discuss how a day of rest can re-fresh, re-focus and re-fuel us. You may be a bit skeptical about whether more rest is even possible in your situation. I invite you to let the Holy Spirit reveal His Truth to you as we investigate some powerful Biblical principles that are often overlooked. Congratulations on having the courage to consider what may seem impossible.

If God took a day off, why can't you?

Following each chapter, there are questions for you to consider. As a life-coach, I have seen the positive results that come from teaming new awareness with new actions. So share the book with a family member, friend, co-worker or group at church and discuss how taking time to rest can and will change your life.

Would you allow me the honor of praying with you as we begin our journey together?

Lord, I thank you that You have initiated this journey for us to discover the possibilities of enjoying a day of rest in You. I stand with every person that has been led to pick up this book. Ease the burdens that are weighing on them.

I ask You to give us a fresh grace to consider what You want to reveal in the middle of our circumstances.

In Jesus' name
Amen

Personal Reflection

When you hear the word *Sabbath*, what do you think of?

How would it feel to give yourself a regular day of rest?

In what ways may God already be placing opportunities for rest in front of you?

1 Good is not always God

Two lumberjacks set out, as they did every morning, to work in the forest. The younger lumberjack challenged the older man to a contest to see which of them could bring down the most trees that day. As soon as the whistle blew, the youth began chopping furiously and built an early lead while his opponent stopped regularly to take a break.

Puzzled by his opponent's unusual strategy, the young lumberjack pressed forward. As the day wore on, he continued chopping as fast as ever, but his lead wasn't what it once had been. It seemed that whatever work he did while the other man rested, was equaled as soon as he got back to work.

When the whistle blew, the challenger, exhausted and in pain from pushing himself all day, turned with astonishment to offer his congratulations to the older lumberjack. Approaching the veteran he said, "I don't get it. I worked all day long without a break, yet in spite of taking several breaks, you still won. What's your secret?"

The veteran, still in good spirits and ready to head home to his family, glanced at the enormous pile of trees he had felled. He replied with a grin, "Son, I wasn't just sitting. I was sharpening my ax."

Mixing wisdom with effort

*"If the ax is dull, And one does not sharpen the edge,
Then he must use more strength;
But wisdom brings success."*
　　　　　　　　　　　　Ecclesiastes 10:10 (NKJV)

Too often we feel ineffective and unsure of what we should be doing. When I was single, I would feel guilty for resting while my married friends were overwhelmed with all they had to do. I loved to serve others and help meet their needs, but I would often find myself offering to assist out of a false sense of obligation.

"For ye have the poor always with you…"
　　　　　　　　　　　Matthew 26:11a (KJV)

The word *poor* is the Greek word ptochos meaning: one who lacks something.

There will always be pressing needs surrounding us, but this does not mean that God wants us to meet all those needs. Instead, we are to stay closely connected to Him at all times so that we are ready, willing and able to be led by Him, to be used as He sees fit – directly or indirectly.

Over the last couple of years, I have been an advocate for a wonderful foster/adoption agency, Family Link. My husband, Eric, and I have aways wanted to adopt, but have not felt it is our time just yet. Instead, God has allowed me the privilege of serving orphans in another way, as an advocate. I've been able to impact more orphans than I ever imagined by sharing with others about the great opportunities available to help nurture these precious children.

We must not ignore needs. Instead, we can be willing to allow God to use us in the manner that He chooses; whether it's meeting the needs directly, or prayerfully looking for those who can.

The proper pace

Within the first six years of our marriage, Eric and I had three beautiful and energetic little boys while serving in the ministry together. And as if that weren't enough, I continued to try to fulfill every need I got wind of. I enjoyed serving within the local church and community because of my passion for teaching and mentoring. Yet, too often I'd race through my Bible, gathering material for ministry purposes and squeeze in just enough time for my appointments. Allowing God to replenish me was not on the schedule. I merely coasted along in cruise control, heading towards empty.

Thankfully I continued to experience the Lord's goodness through the encouragement of the people He placed in my life. But even that was not enough for me to escape the fact that I would not be able to continue the roller-coaster life I was living.

During this season, I remembered a conversation I had with one of my instructors at Fuller Theological Seminary. After witnessing several of my attempts to fill every need I became aware of, he pulled me aside and said, "Andrea, this is a marathon, not a 40 yard dash."

I still remember the concern on his face as he spoke those words to me. That's the moment I began my journey to achieve better balance in my life.

Good can be the enemy of the best

"A false balance is abomination to the LORD: but a just weight is his delight."
Proverbs 11:1 (KJV)

The word *abomination* in Hebrew is tow 'ebah meaning disgusting thing, thing made impure.

Did this mean that the good things I was running around doing for the Lord were seen by Him as an abomination because they shifted my life out of balance?

As a natural do-er, I am more inclined to tackle an activity than sit quietly with the Lord. Even in writing this book on the Sabbath rest, I had to discipline myself to first seek the Lord before doing other things. In order for any of us to discern what is best, we must spend regular time meditating on His word, with His people and in His presence.

Many of us feel a responsibility to live by the motto: "See the need and take the lead." Over the last sixteen years, serving in the church and community, I've seen the endless sea of needs and wants. They never end – kind of like the laundry at my house.

I believe God looks at our hearts and is honored by the desire that we have to serve Him. Yet I wonder why we keep racing toward each finish line as though it is the last, barely stopping to refuel before we start the next race.

We must allow God to fill us first. In this way, we give to others from our overflow, rather than from the grace that is meant to sustain us through the day.

As a life coach, I feel it is beneficial for you to take a few minutes and identify where you are right now and where you need and want to go:

How satisfied are you with the time and energy that you invest in each of the areas listed on the chart below?

Use a pencil to rate each area of your life on a scale from 1-7, with 7 being the highest.

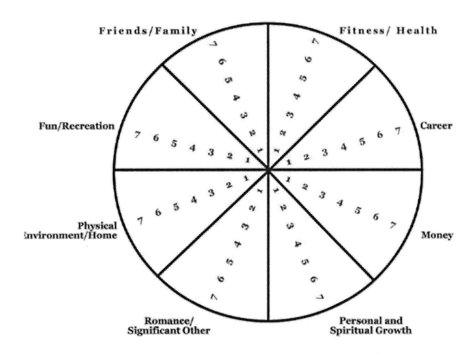

Draw a line connecting your 'score' in each section to the next one, working your way through all eight areas. This will reveal your current state of balance. (Please feel free to change the headings if there are others more applicable to you.)

You can return to this exercise later and modify your wheel as you begin to implement a Sabbath.

As you experience regular rest in the Lord, expect your results to change.

God Took a Day Off, Why Can't I?

As I take a regular Sabbath, areas of my life are going through a transformation, and I'm not seeing the kinds of problems I feared in taking a regular day off.

BONUS: There are two additional wheels in the back of the book as a gift to you. You can chart yourself, either now or later; include where you wish you were or even how your time is being invested once you incorporate a regular Sabbath.

Personal Reflection

In what areas of your life do you want better balance, and what steps can you take to accomplish this?

Are there any "good" things in your life that may not have been initiated by God? If yes, what benefits do you get from pursuing these things?

What steps could you put in place so that you are led by "God" ideas and not just "good" ideas?

Why we need rest

Do you remember the Blue Laws? Everyone had to finish their shopping by Saturday evening, because all major stores were closed on Sundays to support religious practices throughout our country. This national law was eventually removed because of complaints that they were hindering economic growth.

Did removing the Blue Laws improve our economy? Is our country stronger now that businesses are open everyday of the week? Or is that extra day exacting a more personal cost?

Is there a correlation between these two events?

-**Prayer** was removed from our public school system and **crime increased.**
-The **Blue Laws** were removed and **stress** drastically increased.

Stressed out

There are numerous surveys and studies confirming that occupational pressures and fears are a leading source of stress for American adults. Furthermore, these studies show that stress levels have increased steadily over the past few decades. (Caplan, 2010)

The American Institute of Stress (AIS, 4/ 2010) reported that:
- 62% of workers routinely find that they end the day with work-related neck pain.
- 44% reported eye stress.
- 38% complained of hand pain.
- 34% reported difficulty sleeping because of high stress.
- 29% yelled at co-workers because of workplace stress.

Our epidemic of long hours at the office, even if we "office" at home, defies historical precedent and common sense. Many people complain of feeling weary from long days, a lack of sleep, and increasing levels of stress.

> **Sleep**
>
> 40% of American adults get less than seven hours of sleep on weekdays, reports the National Sleep Foundation, up from 31% in 2001. (Mandel, 2005)

Additionally, Dr. Mehmet Oz and many other health professionals have stated that increased stress may be directly contributing to our increased risk of obesity, fatigue and depression.

And yet we are acting like supermen and superwomen, flying straight into the face of all these risks while remaining convinced that we can endure to the end and be okay.

> "Back when we were cavemen and women, stress was a good thing, a fleeting rush of hormones that helped prepare us for impending threat. The prolonged, high-intensity stress so many of us experience today serves no purpose. It only damages our health in the long run, putting us at greater risk for heart problems, cancer, depression, and anxiety and worsens other conditions such as diabetes, asthma and arthritis." (Oz, 2010)

We are no longer living in caves, so it is time for us to get regular breaks and take better care of ourselves.

No one is immune

The church body has also been impacted by stress. An increasing number of spiritual leaders are experiencing burnout. Others resort to just going through the motions, living without the passion that once propelled them out of bed each day.

Stress, with its accompanying mental and physical exhaustion, can cause us to lose our ability to stand firm on our convictions. When we're tired and facing moral dilemmas, we often opt for instant gratification instead of taking the time to think about the consequences of our actions. We simply choose to see how we feel when a problem or situation arises, rather than doing what we know is right.

> **Mealtimes**
>
> About 60% of us are sometimes or often rushed at mealtime, and one-third wolf down lunch at our desks, according to a survey by the American Dietetic Association. (Mandel, 2005)

Most of us are running on fumes and juggling too many obligations. Our tasks keep us so bogged down that we simply don't feel we can stop long enough to get with God.

I remember the zeal that compelled me to witness with people anywhere, even at a gas pump after a conversation began with a warm smile. When I'm out of energy, I'm less likely to share about Jesus with the people I encounter throughout my day.

> **Work-week**
>
> The average work-week has increased, while individual productivity and creativity within the workforce has decreased. (Mandel, 2005)

Dr. Caroline Leaf, author of *Who Switched Off My Brain?* states that, "No system of the body is spared when stress is running rampant." (Leaf, 2009)

Everyone needs a rest

The more I learned about the Sabbath, the more I realized I had a lot of misconceptions regarding working hard and resting. I used to secretly think that people who protected their day off were weak and unable to handle their life's demands, or just rested because *they* needed it. Well, it turns out that they did! After experiencing my own physical and spiritual exhaustion, I realized we all need rest. Everyone needs to regularly hide away with God.

We have compromised our convictions and settled for busyness instead of effectiveness. We are moving too fast to have a clear perspective on our involvement in so many different tasks. God created us to live with a sense of freedom, but His intentions are for us to remain within His boundaries so that He can order our days.

> *Multi-tasking*
>
> To avoid wasting time, we're talking on our cell phones while rushing to work, answering e-mails during conference calls, waking up at 4 a.m. to call Europe, and generally multi-tasking our brains out. (Mandel, 2005)

> *"Lord, teach us to number our days,*
> *That we may present to You a heart of wisdom."*
>
> Psalm 90:12 (NASB)

The word *number* in Hebrew is mannah meaning: to count, assign, appoint, and prepare.

Lord, I pray You will help us pull out of the rat race where we keep running and running as though the needs and events will one day stop. Teach us to allot, assign, make ready and prepare our days for You and not just our own agenda. Show us how to order our days by faith and not just based on pure facts or our perceived reality.

Help us give ourselves permission to rest in You, especially when we have done our part and things are still not perfect. Let us see Your hand and treasure the miracles You perform when we obey and yield our wills to You.

Reveal to us how we can rest in You as our Friend, Father and the only true SUPERMAN! Help us to see our need and let You take the lead as we rest in You.

In Jesus' name
Amen!

Personal Reflection

How do you handle stress and pressure?

What does it take for you to rest right now?

In what ways are you wearing a superhero cape that God desires to wear for you?

What do you fear will happen if you take a whole day off?

If God were to speak to you regarding your fears, what do you think He would say? (*Pause and listen before you answer.*)

3 What is a Sabbath?

*"The Sabbath was made for man,
not man for the Sabbath."*

Mark 2:27 (NIV)

There have been many debates about what a Sabbath is, what activities are permitted, and who should participate. The Sabbath was given to us as a gift from God. It isn't God's checklist for your day off. It's an opportunity for reflection and realignment. The Sabbath is *for you*. God knows we need to rest even if we don't.

We were, after all, made in His image, and the very last thing he created was a day of rest. He took a day off as an example to us and to encourage us to grant ourselves permission to take a breath.

Since the Sabbath is a gift, it should be enjoyed. To do that, we must first know its function. Before we begin, I thought it would be fun to list the top 10 reasons why I think we have a hard time keeping the Fourth Commandment.

"Remember the Sabbath day, to keep it holy."
Exodus 20:8 (NKJV)

The Top 10 Excuses People Give for Not Keeping the 4th Commandment:

(10)
A Sabbath rest is just a state of mind.

(9)
That was just a ritual for the old days.

(8)
I don't need it, but I always make sure I take a "day off" from the office.

(7)
That's what lazy, unmotivated people do.

(6)
I'm too overwhelmed and way too busy to stop.

(5)
I have a family and a very full schedule.

(4)
I have no time to rest.

(3)
There's no way God could expect us to keep that one.

(2)
I would feel so guilty.

NUMBER 1 REASON IS...
A what?!? I never really thought about it. What is it?

What is a Sabbath?

I must be honest – I had a hard time remembering the 10 Commandments. What about you? It's not something that comes up often in conversation. So it's understandable that very few of us would know what the Fourth Commandment is, much less obey it. Before reading ahead, can you list any of the 10 Commandments? How about in order?

1. _____

2. _____

3. _____

4. _____

5. _____

6. _____

7. _____

8. _____

9. _____

10. _____

If Charlton Heston worked so hard bringing those tablets down off that mountain, not once but twice, in the movie *The Ten Commandments*, we should at least look at them.

The 10 Commandments
Exodus 20

1. You shall have no other gods before Me.
2. You shall not make an idol for yourself.
3. You shall not take the name of the Lord your God in vain.
4. Remember the Sabbath day, and keep it holy.
5. Honor your father and your mother.
6. You shall not murder.
7. You shall not commit adultery.
8. You shall not steal.
9. You shall not bear false witness against your neighbor.
10. You shall not covet anything that belongs to your neighbor.

The first three are related to our relationship with God. The last six refer to our relationships with others. The fourth one is what we are discussing – the bridge between God and man.

I find it interesting that God requires a Sabbath rest in Exodus 20, and yet it's such a disregarded topic. If keeping the Sabbath is one of the Ten Commandments, then why aren't we observing it? We have no problem saying that murder is wrong or agreeing that worshipping a golden cow we just constructed probably isn't the best idea, but what about the Fourth Commandment?

Nearly all of the other commandments are obvious when they're being broken, and in each it's clear who is being sinned against. We're not only dishonoring God when we forget our weekly rest, and we're not immediately harming those around us when we don't keep the Sabbath holy. The issues that arise out of ignoring this instruction are more subtle because we're delivering a self-inflicted wound.

Remember the Sabbath...

The word *remember* in Hebrew is zakar meaning: establishing a memorial.

God instructs us to remember the Sabbath. Cultures create memorials to perpetually honor something that's important to them. God directs us to treat our Sabbath the same way.

...and keep it holy.

God says we should keep the Sabbath holy, which always seemed like such an abstract concept to me. What does it mean to keep something holy? Even more, what does it mean to say that something *is* holy? Turns out, it's as simple as setting something apart.

A friend of mine loves dessert so much that he doesn't like to finish dinner and then put the sweets right down on the table. At his house, they clean up after the meal and then come back later to enjoy dessert. By setting it apart, his family has made dessert holy, in the same way that separating ourselves from our regular schedule makes the Sabbath holy.

So, what is a Sabbath?

The word *Sabbath* comes from the Hebrew shebeth or shabbat meaning: to rest, cease, take away, desist from labor, sit still, interrupt, restrain and intermission.

I'll be discussing most of these terms in depth throughout the book, but I want to address a couple of them right away, especially the idea of *restraint*, because it really helped me keep a good attitude about resting, when all I wanted to do was keep going.

Restrain means to limit, restrict, or keep under control. On my day of rest, I actively exercise self-control in order to keep from exerting myself physically. As I restrain myself from participating in regular activities on my day off, I discover how *unrestrained* I have been, continuously wrestling between work and rest on my Sabbath.

The next term is *intermission*. I love all of the words that explain a Sabbath, but the idea of it being an intermission really intrigues me.

Imagine you're in the audience watching a play, when just as you begin to identify with a character's plight, the lights go up, the curtains close and the intermission begins. It doesn't matter how much you want to know what happens next. The pause button has been pressed, and intermission has begun.

That is the Sabbath. You might want to stay right in the nitty-gritty of your to-do list, and there may be a number of things that you really want to see resolved right away, but... it's intermission! When you have committed to set aside this time, you place everything else on the back burner and leave it in God's hands.

I am learning to celebrate the Sabbath by protecting my special time to rest and sit still before the Lord. As I *restrain* myself from moving forward and observe this regular intermission, I find it impacts every area of my life.

When having a conversation with my husband, I will often turn down the volume on other noises (television, radio, etc.). This enables me to savor every word spoken. In the same way, my Sabbath has become a regular opportunity to avoid the distractions of life so that I can be sure not to miss a single word God shares with me.

My Sabbath miracle

Having a regular day where I cease from exertion, rest in the Lord and get refreshed has changed my life. I now have fresh enthusiasm and an overwhelming peace that carries me through the week. I place all of my concerns in His hands while I step back from my regular routine. Witnessing how God handles it all is my Sabbath miracle.

Personal Reflection

What is your reason for not taking advantage of the Sabbath?

In what ways could your lack of scheduled rest be affecting you and those around you?

Why do you think God sometimes calls us to a deeper place with Him?

Which of these meanings for Sabbath speaks loudest to you?

Intermission

Interrupt

Rest

Sitting still

Restrain

In what ways could you "turn the volume down" one day a week?

4 What a Sabbath looks like

"So the sons of Israel shall observe the sabbath, to celebrate the sabbath throughout their generations as a perpetual covenant."

Exodus 31:16 (NASB)

The Sabbath was meant to be a covenant: a never-ending connection between His people and Himself. In a covenant, both sides give freely to the other out of their own abundance. In this case, God is ready to give us productivity, rest and clarity in exchange for our frustration, exhaustion and confusion. Not a bad trade, huh?

When I began studying the Sabbath, I met a lovely Jewish believer who inspired me. She spoke of the Sabbath as something to be celebrated and not just scheduled.

Celebrating the Sabbath requires me to look at it differently; less like a house arrest and more like an opportunity to enjoy special time with a friend. It means that I am not just deciding to obey His command; I'm choosing to rejoice in His invitation to rest.

The transition from running at full throttle to drifting gently downstream isn't always a comfortable one when there's so much left to get done. Feeling like you need an immediate recharge of your batteries, but being required to take an entire twenty-four hours off, often seems absurd and illogical. So let's take a closer look at how the Bible defines a Sabbath, to get a glimpse into God's mindset on this whole day-off thing.

Exodus 23:12 (NASB) says, *"Six days you are to do your work, but on the seventh day you shall **cease from labor** so that your ox and your donkey may **rest**, and the son of your female slave, as well as your stranger, may **refresh** themselves."*

Cease

The word *cease* in Hebrew is shabath meaning to rest, stop from exertion, celebrate, be still, or take away.

The word *shabath* is the same word *Sabbath* comes from. The concept is introduced in verse 11, when God instructs his people to let their land rest every seven years and not plant anything.

I **love** this. It's a beautiful picture of the value of a Sabbath. Like land that must lie fallow so that it's not stripped of nutrients, we must cease from labor so that we aren't depleted. They took a year off from planting crops. We have a full day where all that's on the agenda is resting, recharging and reconnecting with God.

The Israelites had faith that God would support them with enough food to take them through an entire year without a harvest. Likewise, we must believe that our lives will not just endure, but prosper as we follow His commandment to rest. We can accomplish this by delaying our errands, avoiding distractions and ignoring the pull to work from home so that we can set apart a special day with Him.

What a Sabbath looks like

During a recent visit to Houston, I had the opportunity to go walking with a friend. She'd recently become an avid walker after losing over 50 pounds speed walking 3-5 miles every morning. At first, a walk sounded lovely, and quite inspiring considering her incredible physical transformation. As I was getting dressed to go walking, I began thinking about the fact that the walk was interrupting my Sabbath.

My husband was there to watch the kids, so they would have been fine. But I knew that right about mile marker number two, I would hit a wall, the athlete in me would kick in, and I would have to find a way to press through. No way could I allow my friend to completely leave me behind, with her new physically-fit attitude. What began as a great opportunity to be outside would quickly turn into the last leg of a mile relay. I would definitely have to tap into major adrenaline to survive her intense walk. As I weighed the fun I'd have on the walk, versus the joy I experience when I rest through my entire Sabbath, I declined the offer and chose to cease.

Now, I am not saying that walking on your Sabbath is bad. I have zero desire to tell you what to do and what not to do. I just know that for me, working out on my Sabbath does not constitute a day of drawing back or *ceasing from exertion*. It is my one day to not rely on adrenaline. I've found that, if I plan ahead, I can schedule opportunities to exercise on other days, so I don't end up making the Sabbath my opportunity to prepare for swimsuit season.

Rest

The word *rest* in Hebrew is nuwach meaning: to sit, repose, remain, draw breath, or be quiet.

When we operate at such a busy pace, sometimes it's difficult to stop and sit quietly. We might cease, but that's only because we've collapsed on the couch, or we're stuck in front of the TV out of sheer exhaustion. We rarely explore the rest that's possible when we simply sit and remain quiet. We choose to make it difficult rather than seeing it as a reward from God.

I often watch my children as they scurry around. Whether they have a toy or not, they find ways to be active. They wiggle and fidget, run and wrestle. So when it's time for them to rest, I know there's going to be a bit of a delay. We act the same way, until we take action to keep restlessness from being a way of life.

I recently heard from a friend who'd just experienced her first Sabbath. She was full of joy. After years of being convinced that her life was too busy to take a day off each week, she ceased from her tasks and rested. During her Sabbath, she received greater clarity in areas of her life where she had been seeking answers, and it all occurred as she chose to remain quiet.

She'd been wanting to re-decorate a particular room in her home, but in the midst of a full life she was never able to decide just what to do with it. During her Sabbath, she had several special moments with the Lord, but the one that really impacted her was when she received, in an instant, a vivid picture of exactly what she should do with that room. She was thrilled because, along with the perfect solution to one of her concerns, God had shown how much He cared about the things that were important to her.

He knows how we function most effectively. The Sabbath is a day that allows us to receive a fresh and clear perspective, in addition to being a day of rest.

What a Sabbath looks like

Refresh

The word refresh in Hebrew is נָפַשׁ meaning: to take a breath; especially when weary.

God made the world in six days, and then He did something you wouldn't expect of the omniscient, all-powerful designer of every living thing: He took a day off.

I think most people are familiar with the account of creation in Genesis, and in the second chapter it says "He rested" using the same word *shabath* (to cease) discussed earlier in this chapter. But there's a bit more to the story.

When describing this rest God took, Exodus 31:17 says that He ceased from labor... and took a breath (*naphash*) or refreshed Himself. Now, I can't picture God being out of breath, but the idea of Him *taking* a breath makes me stop and think. There is no lack in Him, and yet he paused, and rested, to be an example and to show us how important resting is to Him.

Resting is not an end in itself; God wants us to hear His voice more clearly, which is easiest to do when we're still. He desires to breathe life into us and direct us, but that's difficult to do when we're rushing around, sending Him a prayer for every concern we have before we're off yet again to chase another goal or fix another problem.

Can you imagine God telling you (or even commanding you) to take a day each week where you have His permission to do no work at all? Well, it's not just that He tells us to do it, He did it Himself. He completed His work, and then He took a breath. He refreshed Himself, and He wants to do the same for you.

God Took a Day Off, Why Can't I?

Here is an encouragement from Pastor Laura; a mentor and friend who inspires me weekly to love Jesus and love His people. Pastor Rob & Laura are our pastors at Shoreline Church and we deeply value the life they live so beautifully, all for His glory.

Real Refreshment

"Relax and rest. God has showered you with many blessings"
Psalm 116:7(MSG)

Our *"speed of light"* pace of life has literally worn us out and kept us from experiencing God's true Sabbath rest. We tend to worry and stress, kick our adrenal glands with caffeine, and cram down the wrong foods, i.e. foods high in salt, sugar and fat – all of which keep us going... yet we don't give our bodies what they really need... real refreshment. Eventually, our strong, fearfully and wonderfully made bodies quit, and we end up overwhelmed, exhausted and unable to carry out the amazing purpose that God intended for us. Even worse, we may end up with chronic fatigue, heart disease or other illnesses. All because we simply didn't take the time to rest and relax appropriately. George McDonald said, "If Jesus pressed stillness into a storm, order into the being of a demon-possessed man, health into a desperately sick woman, and life into a dead friend, so He also seeks to press peace into the harried private world of a man or woman who has been in the marketplace all week."

In order to live a joy-filled, peace-permeated, health-saturated life, our family enjoys what we call the 777 plan:

- Every 7 days – we devote one day to true rest.
- Every 7 weeks – we take a long weekend type mini-break.
- Every 7 months – we go on a vacation.

Let's try our best not to work on the Sabbath; but whatever we do -let's enjoy real refreshment!

Dr. Laura Koke, Author of *Fit For The King*, Co-Pastor of Shoreline Church, Loved to Love

Personal Reflection

During your Sabbath, what would it look like for you to:

Cease from exertion?

Rest in the Lord?

Be refreshed by God?

5 Our birthmark

> *"It is a sign between Me and the sons of Israel forever; for in six days the LORD made heaven and earth, but on the seventh day He ceased from labor, and was refreshed."*
>
> Exodus 31:17 (NASB)

The first time a mother holds her newborn in her arms is a moment unlike any other she has ever experienced. That's how it was for me when I got to cradle my little EJ. He looked nothing like me, (definitely his daddy's twin!) yet as I held him, I saw that he had a birthmark on his back just like mine. It was a sweet moment for me as a new mom. My baby had my marking – what a beautiful sign of his connection to me, his mama.

Similarly, our Sabbath rest is a mark of our connection to God. In Exodus 31:17 God calls the Sabbath a *sign*. It is a distinguishing mark to the world, notifying everyone that we are His and that He intends to care for us.

The Israelites had been Egyptian slaves for hundreds of years, and God wanted to create a new culture for them that would identify them as His. He wanted them to have their own unique feature that set them apart as His children. What if you were a spy looking to see what those Israelites were doing after their dramatic departure from Egypt?

Imagine watching them working diligently for six days, but on the seventh day to see nothing... No activity. No work. No movement to speak of. It must have been quite peculiar, yet powerful, to see the Lord's blessing and provision for His people. God had placed His mark on them to make them stand out from all the other nations in the world.

> Can you picture an entire community at rest, enjoying the Lord? What would you think if you saw that?

As I celebrate a regular Sabbath, I see God complete so much on my behalf. And He does so without my involvement. I don't have to feel the heavy weight of ensuring that things don't fall apart while I skip a day. Instead, I am reassured of God's commitment to complete His intentions in and through my life.

As I am being refreshed, my life is filled with peace and a great sense of fulfillment. Others are inspired as they witness the distinguishing mark that God places on us as He draws us to Himself.

I receive fresh Godly perspective and insight in both my personal and work responsibilities. Much like the lumberjack story in Chapter One, my productivity is increasing in many ways because of God's incredible blessing and fresh clarity. I am no longer fighting through the fog that I used to operate under because of exhaustion. My workload has not decreased, but its impact on me and my perspective surrounding it have changed drastically.

I work hard and have high expectations for myself. Yet the more I am able to pull back and receive God's peace and perspective

Our birthmark

on matters, the less I feel forced to do. I am reminded that I was created to be different, but that difference is not based on my works but on what He produces in and through me.

Consequences of removing the mark

"Therefore you are to observe the sabbath, for it is holy to you. Everyone who profanes it shall surely be put to death; for whoever does any work on it, that person shall be cut off from among his people.

For six days work may be done, but on the seventh day there is a sabbath of complete rest, holy to the Lord; whoever does any work on the sabbath day shall surely be put to death."

Exodus 31:14-15 (NASB)

Why does God repeat Himself here, and what wisdom can we find with further study of verses 14 and 15?

The word *death* in Hebrew is muth meaning: to perish or die prematurely by neglect of wise moral conduct.

Now I am not trying to scare you into getting regular rest. I'm just drawing attention to what the Bible says. If scare tactics were effective, we would probably be resting more already because of the signs we've received from doctors, friends, family, and even our own bodies. However, there is clearly a correlation between how we treat our bodies, and what God is saying about premature death.

> 75-90% of sickness and disease is attributed to stress. (AIS, 8/2010)

Physical illness is often the result of our bodies being pushed too hard for too long. We routinely work without stopping, instead of pausing to plug in to the ultimate recharging source.

Many Christians are slowly falling back into old patterns and lifestyles. We are being held back by our health and tripped up by hidden sin that we haven't allowed God to fully deal with. It is harder to resist temptation when we are physically and spiritually fatigued. Yet we are often too busy keeping up the fast pace that our culture admires. In order to celebrate a regular Sabbath, you will have to rely upon supernatural provision that comes with being *marked* by the King.

Personal Reflection

If spies were watching you, what would they see: someone stressed, someone working smart, someone fearful, someone in faith trusting in One greater than themselves?

In what ways is God revealing His desire for you to experience greater rest? As you let Him guide you, in what ways will you be looking for God to provide?

How would regular rest improve your health and well-being?

If you could pull away and celebrate the Lord each week, which areas of your life would you have the hardest time interrupting?

6 How I spend my Sabbath

> *"Let no one act as your judge
> according to food or drink or
> in respect to a festival or a new
> moon or a Sabbath."*
>
> Colossians 2:16 (NASB)

My husband, Eric, is the Worship Pastor at our church. So while Sundays are a wonderful day for many to celebrate the Sabbath, ours are spent in service of others. That's why I celebrate my Sabbath on a weekday, and it works well for our lifestyle. I see God part the waters every week to make my Sabbath miracle happen.

I'm often asked, during coaching sessions and after speaking engagements, what it is that I do on my Sabbath. While I am always happy to talk about it, I make sure to stress that my day of rest is uniquely mine. Please keep that in mind as you read this chapter. You may find some ideas that you like, and others that you don't, but most of all I pray that God helps you discover what *your* Sabbath will look like.

First steps

When I began to consider the Sabbath, it took me a few weeks to try and figure out how I could carve out even a few hours, much less an entire day. At the time, I'd been wanting an *extra* day to work, so I sure didn't feel that I had one to spare!

It was a challenge to even imagine being able to take a day off, so Eric and I prayed and asked God for wisdom.

I considered various activities that I could do ahead of time. We began to get into a routine of taking care of the dishes, and trying to have things picked up so that there would be fewer incomplete tasks silently begging us to work on them. Others may be tempted to just veg-out on a Sabbath, but I always want to get things done. So, I considered things like laundry, phone calls, email, deadlines that might distract me, and a few days ahead of time I began adjusting my routine to get tasks out of the way.

While it didn't happen overnight, I gradually began to walk out of the unrest I was living in. I had to quiet myself, pull back and then get comfortable in it, fighting through the desire to always be doing something.

I told supportive friends and family what I was doing. They respected my decision by not calling or scheduling things for that day. Some went as far as to pray for me on my Sabbath. I was so blessed.

I had to deal with feelings of guilt because I was resting while others worked. At first my mind kept returning to all those unfinished tasks, but I chose to persevere; obeying God no matter what. I realized that God was teaching me a greater level of faithfulness during the week, making the rest day possible. Whatever was left undone, I simply had to entrust to Him.

It wasn't easy to stop relying on busyness. It required a conscious effort to change my mindset, to be able to give myself permission to press the "pause" button, explore and enjoy the Sabbath. But thank God, it happened.

My recipe for rest

Within a few weeks, my special day took on a rhythm of its own. Here's what my typical Sabbath consists of:

The night before my Sabbath, I take some time in the evening to answer emails and deal with any issues that need my attention. Afterwards, I start winding down, emptying my mind of thoughts about needs or projects calling for my attention. Instead of considering things I will tackle the next day, I begin to quiet myself by praying, reading my Bible or sometimes going to bed early. In the morning, I usually begin my time with the Lord journaling, reading my Bible, worshipping (singing or listening to worship music) and studying whatever I am interested in without feeling rushed. Or, if I've already spent a good amount of time studying scriptures earlier that week, then I may not read the Bible much at all.

I find it quite rewarding to just sit and meditate on anything God stirs within my heart. Sitting quietly, I have all the time I need to talk to the Lord. I ask Him to show me what is on His heart regarding me, my marriage, my family, and anyone on my mind that particular day.

I enjoy coming to the Lord with no agenda; just seeing what happens and what He speaks to me as we stop together. I find rest as He reveals His desire to work on my behalf in all that concerns me. The healing, hope, and peace that I experience while I rest doesn't just remain a Sabbath thing. Those moments impact my life throughout the week, and beyond.

Another delightful aspect of taking a Sabbath is being able to take a nap whenever I desire. That's a sweet luxury not to be despised. It is a day of rest after all! At first, I celebrated my Sabbath while my kids were at school and then got back into our regular work mode once I picked them up. As I became more comfortable with not being busy, I began drawing back a bit from our regular routine. We gradually changed our after-school activities, limited play-dates, and stopped running around to catch up on errands.

Now, after I've picked up the kids from school, we come home, do homework, eat a meal that I typically have prepared beforehand (or go out to eat) and then just keep things low key. We sometimes play puzzles, read, listen to worship music, chat, or just enjoy being together for a little bit of down time before bed. We simply celebrate this day with the volume of life turned down.

After the kiddos are tucked into bed, Bible stories are read, and all their prayers are prayed, I often resume a final peaceful moment either reading my Bible, flipping through a magazine, enjoying a book, or watching a movie before going to bed – usually a bit earlier than I do the rest of the week.

Magazines, movies, and things like that are a rare treat for me because I usually don't stop to indulge in them. If I did, then I probably would avoid them on my Sabbath. I try to refrain from activities that are a part of my regular entertainment or things that I consider time thieves for me.

I have to be careful not to slip back into work-mode. Sometimes I'll be enjoying my day and slowly my mind will become fixated on a current project. Before I realize it, I have started strategizing and have fallen back into work.

As soon as I recognize what I'm doing, I quickly write down my thoughts for later and resume resting in the Lord.

I exert so much energy into what I do throughout the week, that on my Sabbath I try to not work out or exert myself. I take the day to get spiritually refreshed, but let my body rest as well. It's my one day to take advantage of this, and God makes weekly arrangements for my rest.

I turn off my computer and place my cell phone on vibrate for most of the day (I can still be reached in an emergency on our home phone), and I try to avoid my email and social media sites too. It is so fun the morning after my Sabbath to go to my inbox and see all that God did while I rested.

I also do my best to not get legalistic about my day, and most of the things I've talked about in this chapter are guides for me. There are some rare times when I have a call or appointment that is scheduled for my Sabbath. In those situations, I ask God for guidance. I figure this whole resting thing was His idea, so why not consult with the one who knows it best?

Once I had a meeting I felt should not be cancelled, so I went ahead and kept it while being sure to treat the rest of my Sabbath as I normally would. I felt so much peace about it, and I experienced God's refreshing hand through the whole day – even during the meeting. I don't make it a habit, but it was clear to me that God was guiding me, showing me that His grace would cover these occasional exceptions as I continued to seek Him about how to handle each one.

On my Sabbath, I keep a note pad handy to capture great ideas

God Took a Day Off, Why Can't I?

I get for work, things I need to do, or people I need to contact. I write them down and then I know I can tend to them the next day. This really helps keep me from being distracted by things I'd want to work on. It's much easier to relax when I'm not worried about forgetting something I just thought of.

On Sabbath days when my babies are home, they celebrate with me. We read, talk, sing, play, and just have an enjoyable time as a family. The kids sometimes start dancing, which quickly turns to laughing as I get up to show them how it's done! Just like Eric and me, the kids were reluctant at first, but as they experience the sweet moments within this day, they have quickly grown to appreciate them. I think it's because of the memories we have made. Our family ends up talking, learning, and enjoying each other as we all get re-charged for the week. We don't have a set schedule, or force any kind of agenda on ourselves during the Sabbath. We just allow for opportunities to connect as we celebrate the Lord together.

A picture my son Josiah, a.k.a."King Jo-Jo", drew after enjoying a Sabbath. (A Sabbath he was a bit reluctant to begin!)

Personal Reflection

What stood out to you from this chapter?

What would your ideal Sabbath day look like?

What's your next step in celebrating a Sabbath?

In addition to God, who can support you in this?

7 Overcoming obstacles

"There is no fear in love; but perfect love casts out fear, because fear involves punishment, and the one who fears is not perfected in love."

I John 4:18 (NASB)

We are nearing the end of potty training our youngest, Tre', and it is quite an adventure. I think it's hilarious that he will be in the middle of the "I-have-to-go-potty" dance and run *past the bathroom* to tell us about it. Once he has notified us, and we've redirected him to the restroom, it's as though he's been given permission to give his body relief. All obstacles have been removed and he sees his way clear to deal with his urgent situation.

Likewise, we have obstacles we must overcome to reach our goals. And more often than not, they are internal. Our situation can appear hopeless, or things can seem primed for victory – depending on our mindset. When we stop looking at where we're going, and focus instead on what's in our way, our roadblocks can send us in the wrong direction, away from our answer and right back into the familiar.

That's why I appreciate the verse at the beginning of this chapter so much. What John says about fear, punishment and love shows us the way around our obstacles. Moving past these hindrances will allow us to walk in the freedom of God's love while enjoying the blessings that His ways provide.

Fear

The word *fear* in Greek is phobos meaning: terror or dread.

Fear is a powerful force. It can paralyze us and prevent us from taking a single step in a new direction – even if we detest our current circumstances. Fear can also keep us busy, as if by staying active we can shield ourselves from harm.

> What's your reason for not doing something you feel God wants you to do?

We run away from situations because at the core of fear is the desire to avoid pain or suffering. It is this desire that caused Jesus, as He faced the Cross, to ask God to remove the cup of suffering from Him. (Matt 26:39) But by allowing God to love the world through Him, Jesus overcame fear and became a ransom for many. (Matt 20:28)

Punishment

When John pairs fear with punishment, he's speaking directly to the part of us that loses sight of God's love when we are afraid.

The word *punishment* in Greek is kolasis meaning: correction or penalty.

This is why Jesus' example is so important – He avoided the obstacle of fear by keeping God's love at the center of His focus. There is no reason to expect punishment from the God who *is* love. If we do, then it is a warning to us that we don't fully grasp His love. God's correction is always redemptive. Because God's love is so far beyond our human comprehension, it's easy to believe that it is also beyond our ability to experience. It's not. Simply taking time to sit still in His presence is enough to start the process of growing up in His love. As we grow, that fear will lose its grip on our hearts.

Perfect Love

When I was little, I loved puppet shows. No matter how big or small, those characters would capture my focus as I watched them sing, laugh, and jiggle about. The puppeteers who made them move, however, were invisible – even non-existent, as far as I was concerned.

As I grew older, I began to realize there were areas of my life much like those beloved puppet shows; something hidden was influencing what I saw. I have also come to understand that the hidden influence standing between me and obedience to God is usually fear. Nothing but plain old fear.

So why are we afraid to obey God? Are we afraid we'll miss out on something "better"? Or are we afraid that we won't be good enough, and so we will be under God's correction or scrutiny? We need to work past that, to take ownership of the "perfect love" promised to us in 1 John 4:18. Doing so will carry us past our fears and beyond the things that torment us.

The word *perfect* in Greek is telzios meaning: mature, complete, lacking nothing.

The assurance we receive from His perfect love makes us complete, whether or not a prayer has been answered or a single problem solved. In His love there is **no punishment.** No lack. No penalty. No correction.

When I take time to steep myself in His presence, my worries disappear as I'm infused with His love. It's like a light is turned on in my soul. No matter how dark a room is, when the lights are turned on, the darkness is driven out.

That's what it means for perfect love to cast out fear. There is no battle between the light and the dark when the switch is flipped on; the light shines and the darkness cannot stay.

In Him we experience perfect love. A love that heals, and a love that covers. A love that completes us and equips us to love others. The love we receive in God's presence is what drives away fear. It is not flawed by human frailty or imperfections. The more we spend time in His love, the more we will walk in freedom.

> What types of fears do you face? Fears of loss, fears of failure, fears of rejection, fears of success?

In fact, when we are worried or anxious, it should be a signal to us that we need to get alone with Him, and reconnect with His perfect love. I enjoy reading scripture with the Greek/Hebrew meanings placed within the verse. Let's look at 1 John 4:18 again in this different light: *There is no **dread** in love; but **mature** love casts out **terror**, because **terror** and **dread** involve **punishment**, and the one who fears is not **completed** in love.*

Control

As you consider observing the Sabbath, you may start to worry that your house will fall apart, your business will collapse, or your team will fail without you. Like all of us, you *need* a Sabbath. Expect that God will perform miracles in re-structuring how your household, business (and all the rest of your life) actually works. Don't overlook anything as being beyond His notice, too small, or too large for Him.

Control is often the fruit of deep internal fear. Don't think you have to wait until you figure it all out; that's just another way to control the unknown. Refusing to relinquish control will keep you from walking in all that God has promised for you.

When God leads us into new areas of His provision, He confirms our direction. Do not doubt whether God is leading you into a Sabbath. He has confirmed it repeatedly. The Holy Spirit will guide you, if you will stop and listen to Him.

It is hard for us to allow change when we are holding on, afraid of what we might lose. I often use a word picture in my coaching sessions. When we need to trust the Lord no matter what, we can hold our palms up and away from us. This is such a beautiful sign of yielding, trusting that God will supply. It's like saying, "God, this is precious to me, but I know that You know best. I will hold it away from my heart to be closer to Yours, and I give You the right to do with it what You think is best. I choose to trust You."

Mistrust

Are there any areas you need to entrust to the Lord? I am constantly being shown new parts of my life that God wants me to surrender to Him. I may be hurt in a relationship, then get fed up and decide, "That sure ain't gonna happen again!" I may feel like I've been taken advantage of, so I decide, "I need to look out for me." All of these reactions are normal, but who am I declaring is in charge? ME! Why do I need to be in charge if God loves me so much, wants the best for me, and knows the quickest route to get me there?

Unfortunately, a lack of trust gets in God's way of doing just that. And while we need to turn over to God those things we have been unwilling or unable to give to Him, this is **not** something that He expects us to do on our own. Simply ask Him to help you let it go. The answer He gives you might not be simple, but He'll help you accomplish that too.

Surrender

Every fear, control, and trust issue that's hindering us from yielding, we must bring to Him.

We may not have considered our need to surrender our rights and desires to God. We sometimes forget what makes our relationship with Him so unique, but as we surrender to His Lordship in any area, He is glorified and able to far surpass our expectations.

Surrendering to His Lordship is essential; it is our secret weapon to significant blessing and protection. I enjoy reminding myself that He…

"is able to do immeasurably more than all we ask or imagine, according to His power that is at work within us."

Ephesians 3:20 (NIV)

Lordship

I once heard someone describe our treatment of Christianity like "a buffet line at our favorite restaurant!" We treat our faith like the menu items found in the buffet:

-"I'll take the church on Sundays, but I want it without the tithe."

-"I'll have a serving of no drunkenness, but you better forget it if you think I'm gonna stop shacking up. We are going to get married, anyway!"

-"I'm with you on the no murder, adultery, lying, and stealing bit in the Commandments, but I'm sorry God, I can't do the Sabbath thing. That is just not going to work for me!"

Christ became our Savior when He died on the Cross for our sins nearly 2,000 years ago. He must be our Lord, too. Lord over every area of our lives, including how we rest and play. When we say Jesus is "Lord" it's because He is the one who calls the shots! Some of us have overlooked or forgotten this Truth.

> In the NIV translation, the word 'Lord' is found 7,801 times, while the word 'Savior' occurs only 59 times. Where do you think God wants the emphasis?

Christ's intent in Lordship is not to hinder our lives and careers, or to be an insensitive taskmaster. As we yield to Him, He will surpass our dreams and expectations. We must trust and follow Him as Savior **and** Lord.

On June 18th, 1994, I realized God had a plan for my life, and I surrendered myself to His plan. I no longer wanted to call the shots or make decisions based upon what I felt. I was ready to yield control of my life to Him, and I've never regretted making that decision. He consistently brings hope, healing and help to me as He works all things together for my good. (Romans 8:28)

If you sense a real purpose for your life, yet have never surrendered your life to Him, I would love to lead you in a prayer. I would also like to pray with you if you consider yourself a Christian, yet have been living as though your relationship with God is like a local buffet restaurant where you just pick and choose what you want.

Lord Jesus,

I thank You for drawing me closer to You. I repent of all of my sin that I have committed knowingly and unknowingly, and I choose now to stop trying to be the boss. I ask You to forgive me, and I choose to forgive myself of all my past sins and the repercussions from it all. I lay my fears and insecurities before You, and receive Your grace in their place.

I ask You to come and take Your rightful place as the Lord of every area of my life. I thank You for Your wisdom and grace that will lead me to be who You intended me to be, and enable me to live as You want me to live.

Have Your way in my life, that I may experience knowing You as my Counselor, Friend, Lord, and Heavenly Father.

In Jesus' Mighty Name,

AMEN!

If you prayed this prayer, I encourage you to tell a trusted friend, and ask God to lead you to a local church family. Get help to find a spiritual mentor, so that you will have others to grow and live life with in the Lord.

I want to rejoice with you!

Feel free to email me at Andrea@Hisdesignforsuccess.com

Personal Reflection

What are the roadblocks preventing you from experiencing a regular Sabbath? Once you write them down, pause and listen to what the Holy Spirit speaks to your heart about them.

In what ways are you treating your relationship with God like a buffet line?

How can you relinquish control to God and trust in His commitment to perfect what He has begun in you?

Is there anything that God wants you to yield to His Lordship?

8 Faith to Rest

"There remains, then, a Sabbath-rest for the people of God; for anyone who enters God's rest also rests from their works, just as God did from His."
Hebrews 4:9-10 (NKJV)

It requires faith to regularly celebrate a Sabbath. Life doesn't take a break just because I've scheduled one. The issues surrounding me are often unresolved as I'm settling in to begin my Sabbath.

Initially, I had to ignore my natural tendency to jump right in and start working on these challenges. This was so difficult to do because everything within me wanted to fix my problems as soon as they surfaced. Yet in this new paradigm of resting, I now choose to yield those desires to His will. I entrust the situation into His hands, and then follow Him. I stand in faith behind the God I serve and choose to enter His rest.

As a result, my faith has been increased through the experience of watching God lead me through these uncharted waters.

Where God guides, He provides

"My God will supply all your needs according to His riches in glory in Christ Jesus."
Philippians 4:19 (NASB)

I am in awe of how God takes care of the things that I force myself to overlook. As I put Him and His will first, He provides for me better than I could have myself.

Since beginning my journey:

- God has made a Sabbath rest possible every week that I have simply been willing.
- I've drawn closer to the Lord, as I have had ample opportunity to ask Him what is on His heart and sort through what's in mine.
- God has used me more efficiently, since I feel less obligated to do and more comfortable simply *being*.
- I've watched God go before me regarding contracts, projects, opportunities, and events with my career and personal matters, with much less of my own participation.
- I've felt less guilt over not participating in everything. I have also received greater clarity to serve and to implement strategies resulting in being effective and not just busy.
- I have increased creativity, productivity, and confidence from His working in and through my life while I show up and yield to Him.
- I've experienced God confirming His desire to have a day set apart for our family, by helping us protect it as we celebrate Him.
- The morning after my Sabbath, I am more prepared to work and see what God has done while I rested in Him.

There is absolutely nothing I miss about *not* having a regular Sabbath, and I savor each one uniquely. NOTHING I am responsible for has fallen apart as I have begun to follow God's path for me. Since learning how to regularly rest in Him, everything in my life has gotten better!

By no means am I saying that my life is now perfect, but I have greater clarity, more peace, and I am experiencing more of His grace daily. This journey will require faith in order for you to enter His rest. Please don't be surprised if you have a ton of fresh opportunities and invitations flooding your calendar, fighting for the right to be scheduled on your Sabbath.

> The areas where we experience our greatest challenges are often the places that God is preparing for us to have the greatest impact.

This is a spiritual venture, and there is testing and occasional opposition that you may have to face. We must trust that if the Lord has initiated this new journey for you, then He is ready and prepared for everything that may come your way. Step forward and...

> "Taste and see that the LORD is good;
> Blessed is the man who trusts in Him! Oh, fear the LORD,
> you His saints! There is no want to those who fear Him."
>
> Psalm 34:8-9 (NKJV)

It's easy to blame our environment, spouse, or boss for our inability to stop and pull away with God. These reasons can appear quite valid when we look only at the facts.

But God regularly moves beyond facts and figures to protect what He has entrusted to us. He will make sure that we lack nothing we truly need, if we choose to trust Him.

We must extend our faith beyond our circumstances and yield the possibilities over to Him. God does not want us to be ruled by the needs around us. Nor does He want us to be preoccupied by the idea of the Sabbath, allowing it to weigh us down with one more thing we need to be doing.

Since experiencing a regular Sabbath, I have seen God work many miracles, both in my heart and in my calendar. I am forgetting about less important things that I previously would have felt guilty missing. Other events are getting rescheduled with very little effort or excuse, simply because of my willing heart to honor God, and His response to my obedience. I'm not getting as many phone calls as I used to on my Sabbath. If God can make a way for this mom of three busy young boys, a full family calendar, and a deep passion to help others, He can make a way for you too, even with all the complexities that you face – if you want Him to.

> **Pay it Forward**
>
> When parents are not bogged down and learn how to live a reduced stress life, the children benefit greatly from their choices.

God wants to be invited into the details and obstacles of our lives. Even when we see no possibilities, God can change the intensity of our schedules or give us options for some rest versus none. He can show us ways to begin – somewhere, somehow, and in some way – to carve out a Sabbath rest with Him. This rest brings about lasting change and fresh perspective to all areas of our lives.

A Personal Plea

If you are still having a hard time imagining God making a way for you to take a day off, then take baby steps. Even if you begin on a smaller scale. Just begin! Ask God to show you how to start with a few hours. Practice spending time sitting still, ceasing from exertion, and allowing Him to breathe on you.

> *"Let us, therefore, make every effort to enter that rest, so that no one will perish..."*
>
> Hebrews 4:11 (NKJV)

God **will** provide where He guides. As you experience His blessing and protection, you will desire more, and your faith will help guard it. He will lead the way for you to experience a regular Sabbath Day rest.

> *"Therefore, since the promise of entering his rest still stands, let us be careful that none of you be found to have fallen short of it. For we also have had the good news proclaimed to us, just as they did; but the message they heard was of no value to them, because they did not share the faith of those who obeyed. Now we who have believed enter that rest."*
>
> Hebrews 4:1-3a (NIV)

Personal Reflection

What are the next steps you will take to celebrate a Sabbath?

In what ways are you looking for His provision to make this day a regular celebration?

If you were to begin this week carving out a work-free zone, when would it be? What would it look like?

9 Not a demand, but a delight

Here in Austin, Texas, it is HOT almost all year round. This makes us thankful that Brenham is not too far away to take the occasional trip to sample all the wonders of the Blue Bell Ice Cream Factory.

When we want to go for a quick family outing, we'll head into our local ice cream shop where something happens to me. Initially, I walk into the store with the intent of getting nothing more than a child-sized sugar cone with mint chocolate chip ice cream.

Soon I am mesmerized by the oversized posters of sundaes loaded with nuts that scream, "ANDREA... ANDREA, remember how yummy we are!?!" I gaze at all that hot fudge drenched on top, dripping ever so perfectly over the sides, with a polite cherry resting on top of it all. (You know, I think that cherry gets me to subconsciously believe that I'm making a healthy choice. I wonder what Kratai, my personal trainer, would think!)

All of a sudden, I'm saying, "Babe, I changed my mind. Can you order me a two-scoop mint chocolate chip sundae with whipped cream, nuts, and a cherry? Oh, and hot fudge please, not caramel." Ahhh... pure delight.

God Took a Day Off, Why Can't I?

Well, it's delightful if I don't do it all the time.

Isaiah 58:13-14 (NASB) refers to the Sabbath, and calls it too, a delight:

> *"If because of the sabbath, you turn your foot*
> *From doing your own pleasure on My holy day,*
> *And call the sabbath a delight, the holy day of the LORD honorable,*
> *And honor it, desisting from your own ways,*
> *From seeking your own pleasure*
> *And speaking your own word,*
> *Then you will take delight in the LORD,*
> *And I will make you ride on the heights of the earth;*
> *And I will feed you with the heritage of Jacob your father"*

Let's look a little closer into the meaning behind this passage and see if we can get a little more clarity on God's intent in this scripture.

I have no need for clarity with my experience at the ice cream shop. My delight with my sundae would be found under the same listing, in my heart, as J.J. on the '70s hit TV show Good Times. He often referred to the things he deeply loved as **"Dy-no-mite!!!"**

The word *delight* is used in two slightly different ways within this passage. In doing so, it reveals an intriguing effect that comes from our relationship to the Sabbath.

A Luxury

The word *delight* in Hebrew is `עֹנֶג` meaning: a luxury.

Not a demand, but a delight

God is saying that He wants us to turn from what we normally do throughout the week, and treasure our Sabbath day just like we would something we've saved up for, and rarely get to experience.

When I consider the word luxury, I immediately think of ordering room service as I recline in a Presidential suite at a five star hotel, set in the most beautiful surroundings. Within moments a delicious meal is being placed in front of me, and removed with a mere phone call. There's nothing to clear away, no dishes to do, not even a receipt to sign. Oh, the sheer delight!

> Can you imagine enjoying a day set aside as a luxury on a regular basis?

I approach the Sabbath with just this kind of expectation. My mind is renewed as I delight in the luxury of resting and communing with God. I look forward to it and treasure all that He prepares for me within each one.

Soft and pliable

The word *delight* in Hebrew is עָנֹג meaning: soft and pliable.

The second use of the word *delight* comes from an entirely different word in the original text, which introduces the idea that if we treat this day as a luxury, then we will be soft and pliable before Him.

It's one of those interesting if/then statements in the Bible. In verse 13, God says that *if* we will consider the Sabbath a delight and a luxury by not doing what we want but what He directs, *then* something remarkable will happen. Our hearts "will take delight in the Lord" by becoming soft and pliable. Read on to see what's so great about that.

> If you are having a hard time today, sing songs to the Lord, it'll help your heart soften before Him.

What a soft heart can do

When I was single, a friend told me something that really opened my eyes about having a soft heart. Before she ever met her fiancé, she sat down and wrote out a list of all of the things she desired in her future husband. Once she was engaged, she looked back at the list, and realized that he was everything she had ever desired in a spouse.

I was inspired, so I set out to make my list, too. Before I did, I prayed and read another verse that also mentioned the word *delight* or `*anag* – soft and pliable.

> *"Delight yourself in the Lord;*
> *And He will give you the desires of your heart."*
>
> Psalm 37:4 (NASB)

The word *give* is the Hebrew word נתהן which can mean: to exchange.

So I first made sure that my heart was soft before the Lord. From that place, I sought His desires and presented Him with the things that concerned me. God was then able to give me the desires of my heart, but He did exchange some of mine for His. This was possible because I was willing to accept what He placed within me.

When God promises to give us the desires of our heart, it is with the understanding that our hearts are soft and pliable in His hands. This enables a gentle exchange to happen, from His heart to ours. He then not only gives us the desires of our hearts, but within this gentle exchange, He gives us new desires.

As I got to know Eric, I was amazed, just like my friend had

Not a demand, but a delight

been, by how he surpassed the desires within my heart. It's such a blessing to look back on the way God brought me through that process, yet there's one more piece to this puzzle, and it's in the scripture found directly above, in the third verse.

> *"Trust in the Lord and do good;*
> *Dwell in the land and cultivate faithfulness."*
> Psalm 37:3 (NASB)

The word *dwell* in Hebrew is shakan meaning: to settle down, abide, take rest.

There are times when we wait for just the right circumstances before we move into something new.

The placement of this verse implies that while He's giving us the desires of our hearts, God wants us to rest in Him – to *dwell*. He designed us to be our best as we trust Him with all that concerns us, then settle and abide right where we are.

Let's be carried

The word *ride* in Hebrew is rakab meaning: to be carried, to ride on the wings of the wind.

Learning to honor and delight in the rest that God calls us to, leads us into the ride of our lives. We all experience moments where we feel as though we are alone or that our challenges are too great. This image of being carried is the perfect illustration of how God wants to take us on a ride and carry us through each season. And all we have to do is choose His way, and delight in the Sabbath.

God Took a Day Off, Why Can't I?

Here is a word from another of my mentors, Helen Hall. Helen was the very first person I ever heard share a message on the Sabbath. For the last 18 years, Helen has graciously inspired me in my faith and my personal relationship with the Lord.

A Time of Reflection

When I was growing up, washing clothes was not on the Sunday agenda. My mother considered turning on the washing machine as work. She taught me that the Sabbath was a holy day, and there were certain things she would never do on the Sabbath.

Unfortunately, as an adult, Sunday became just another day filled with other kinds of activities. After church, lunch, and maybe a nap, the day was pretty much gone. Noticing that my life seemed to lack any time for real reflection and rest, I began to study about the Sabbath, wondering if God had more in mind. If He commanded us to prioritize a special day for us to rest, then there must be something intriguing I was missing.

When I considered conventional wisdom, the necessity of this commandment began to make sense. From a human viewpoint, if six days are good for work, surely seven should be even better! We press and push, run and hurry, only to find that there are not enough hours in a day. How easy it is to find ourselves on a treadmill of activity that never seems to stop!

I began to realize it is only in purposefully stepping off the treadmill that I have any hope of re-evaluating my priorities. A day for perspective brings life to my week! For me, this time of reflection became the holy luxury called the Sabbath.

My experiences have taught me that even the greatest purposes and the most valiant causes cannot become an altar on which all else is sacrificed. Sometimes it is not just our flurry of activity that needs to be re-evaluated, but it is our perspective that the glorious end will certainly justify the exhausting means. We have lost the wisdom of God's rest and the supernatural multiplication that He can bring forth from this rest.

Left to myself, I would push until I drop and sadly wonder why God allowed this meltdown to happen. As I seize the Sabbath and embrace a restful day to hear from Him, He offers me a way out. He offers me His perspective to see clearly, and He breathes divine energy into my heart to run the race that He sets before me.

Helen Hall, CEO Energy Venued, Broker/Owner Ambiance Properties

Personal Reflection

In what ways has the Lord been trying to carry you? Have you been resisting or making excuses?

What would it look like for you to treasure the Sabbath as a luxury?

In what ways can you practice keeping your heart soft before the Lord?

What are the desires stirring within your heart? (Take a minute and pray before answering this question)

10 Preparing and protecting

"See, the LORD has given you the sabbath; therefore He gives you bread for two days on the sixth day. Remain every man in his place; let no man go out of his place on the seventh day. So the people rested on the seventh day."

Exodus 16:29, 30 (NASB)

In Exodus 16, we see our very first mention of a Sabbath. Here we read about God providing the manna for the children of Israel as they headed to Mt. Sinai. God helped His children prepare ahead of time for the Sabbath.

When I first considered taking a regular Sabbath, I tried to think ahead as to what this would require. Essentially, I had to change from a very full 7 day week (which felt more like an 8 or 9 day week), to visualizing my active life in 6 days. How could I best prepare and protect this new lifestyle?

I began to make a mental list to get ready for this special day. This list should help you get started with your own Sabbath. While some of the points may not be applicable to you, it will get you thinking about the steps you can take to make this day a reality for you.

Prepare

- I try to plan the day's meals ahead of time. This way I do not have to cook or spend as much time in the kitchen on the Sabbath.
- I schedule appointments, deadlines, and anything administrative either before or after my Sabbath.
- I try to have my dishes all washed and put away the evening before my Sabbath.
- Paper products are great to use, alleviating a pile-up at the end of a Sabbath day.
- I try to have all laundry done and put away the night before, or at least make sure it's out of my sight!

Watch out for distractions

Preparing for the Sabbath is only half the story, you must protect it too. And what you're protecting it from are distractions.

As I began observing a Sabbath, I noticed something that surprised me. In slowing down, I would see my unorganized clothes closet and messy desk in my home office. Or I would think about how amazing my vegetable garden would look if I just applied an hour here or there. Before I knew it, I would find myself straightening up, convinced that it would be so much easier to focus on my time with God, once this task was done.

> Preparation makes the promise possible.

It all seemed so appealing when, for once in my life, I actually had time to take care of something like this. Then I remembered that this precious time was already accounted for – I had set it aside as time to cease from exertion.

It's interesting, almost humorous, how everything changes as you slow down. For most of us, if we stop from our regular fast-paced routine for even a short while, we start feeling fresh motivation to tackle a project, return a phone call, or just casually catch up with a friend.

I admit that resting all day is by no means a natural thing for me, but I've been enjoying a Sabbath for a good while now and I still find that, in the middle of my rest day, I'll switch over into thinking about all the people I need to contact, the things I could be doing, and the opportunities that need to be seized. Great ideas, but it's not a Sabbath if I spend it constantly taking a break, from taking my break.

Be on the look-out for your distractions – even good ones! They are still distractions.

Protecting with boundaries

The best way I've found of dealing with distractions is setting up boundaries. I've already shared my own story of how I protect my day in Chapter 6. Please spend some time to prayerfully consider how you should guard your time on your Sabbath.

What I will do to protect my Sabbath:

- _____
  _____
- _____
  _____
- _____
  _____
- _____
  _____

God has given us the Sabbath as a gift – not to rule over us, but to bless and refresh us.

God Took a Day Off, Why Can't I?

Here is a thought from Pat Lawson. Leo & Pat, a.k.a Gramps & Grammy to our kids, have been such a great encouragement to our family. I thank God for their willingess to teach, inspire, and nurture us in the Lord.

Be Prepared

I can't imagine how hard it must have been for those women who followed Jesus for years to see Him die on the cross one gloomy afternoon. Heartbroken, devastated and distraught, they saw Him taken from that cross and followed at a distance to see where His body was laid (Lk 23:48-55). If I saw that, I probably would have been disheartened and at a loss, not knowing what to do. They knew what to do. They prepared spices to be ready for when they would visit the tomb after the Sabbath! Yet... they were going to take a Sabbath, a day of rest, to keep still and reflect on God's faithfulness. (Lk 23:48-56)

Taking a Sabbath when all is going well is one thing, but it's so hard for me in the midst of uncertainty and bewilderment to take time out to REST and be still. In my frazzled state, when going through some traumatic event, I have to DO something. I see that God is at work on these days, if I simply make room for Him. (PS. 46:10)

These women were prepared to not work, but rest on their Sabbath. They readied their spices and ointments for the NEXT DAY after their Sabbath! Instead of running in circles, they prepared... and then rested.

During the time of their rest, their Father was working (Jn 5:17). They weren't just resting physically but, I believe, resting in God. Thus, they were ready for the next day. Early that Resurrection morning, they came to the tomb prepared. (Lk 24:1)

During my days of resting and refreshing, the Lord stirs the waters of my soul, while healing my body as well. So, much like the man Jesus healed on the Sabbath who had been ill for 38 years (Jn 5:4,8-9), when I feel too weak, He meets me where I am, encourages me, strengthens me, and asks me to pick up my pallet and walk. Whether I'm weak or strong, at a loss or bold, devastated or confident, I will walk forward.

Pat Lawson, Board of Advisors, International Center for Evangelism, Church Planting and Prayer

Personal Reflection

In what ways would you prepare for a regular Sabbath?

What distractions will you have to guard against to protect your Sabbath?

What would change if you knew a regular Sabbath would bring you fresh ideas, thoughts, perspective?

11 Freedom

"As we discover how God wants us to rest, we will then discover how He wants us to live."
Brandon Heath

Sitting still before my Creator on my rest day fills me with an overwhelming sense of peace which anchors me in Him. Peace to let go of things I held on to for security. Peace to sit still without an agenda. Peace to trust that He is GOD. Peace that surpasses all my understanding and guards my heart and mind in Christ Jesus (Philippians 4:7). As I commune with God on our special day, the experience I have during my Sabbath miracle is changing the way I view life.

What He reveals to me during our special day flows over into the rest of the week. I am seeing my perspective on the other 6 days change. Many things I used to feel obligated to do, I now see as simply good ideas, or even opportunities for others! The more I see God move on my behalf, the more my faith grows.

My family's commitments to outside activities have changed. We are less compelled to do, and more able to be a blessing in the things God allows us to take part in. We are being revamped from the inside out.

> *"So teach us to number our days,*
> *That we may present to*
> *You a heart of wisdom."*
>
> Psalm 90:12 (NASB)

The word number in Hebrew is manah meaning: to be divided out, assign, appoint, and prepare.

My faith is growing in the Truth that God wants to "divide out, assign, appoint, and prepare" my days. My world is feeling less cluttered and more appointed. I am not so worried, because I see God go before me. He works out the details much better than I ever could through my own efforts.

I hope throughout this journey you have been considering your own hurdles and challenges, and examining what you have subconsciously believed. No matter where we are on our journey with the Lord, He is never too far. It's never too late, no matter how captive we may feel at work, or in our personal lives.

> How would your life be different, if you felt refreshed and had greater clarity from the One who created you?

Come back to your first love and sit with Him. He was the one who parted the Red Sea and made the sun stand still. He made a donkey speak, the blind see, and the lame walk. He can take care of everything that concerns you. He is calling you to Himself for a reason. Pull away with Him. All that you'll become awaits you, and will be revealed.

Be YOUR Best,

Andrea

Have you prayed to ask God to lead you and show you how to celebrate your Sabbath? If you haven't, why not take the opportunity to do so as you read this Psalm?

Psalm 67

*God be gracious to us and bless us,
And cause His face to shine upon us – Selah.
That Your way may be known on the earth,
Your salvation among all nations.
Let the peoples praise You, O God;
Let all the peoples praise You.
Let the nations be glad and sing for joy;
For You will judge the peoples with uprightness
And guide the nations on the earth. Selah.
Let the peoples praise You, O God;
Let all the peoples praise You.
The earth has yielded its produce;
God, our God, blesses us.
God blesses us,
That all the ends of the earth may fear Him.*

Personal Reflection

What steps have you begun to take in fulfilling the 4th Commandment?

Which parts of the book do you think you should go back and revisit later?

Why?

What obstacles still prevent you from taking a Sabbath?

Acknowledgements

I love living life with others. So, writing this book was no different. I could not have accomplished this project alone. I thank God for His inspiration and guidance to do what I consider more than just an opportunity, but rather a responsibility that He has given me!

There are so many special people to thank, people who have carried me through this project:

My amazing husband and babies... I truly am a blessed woman!

Our parents and siblings who love us in such a wonderful way. Phyllis, I can't wait to enjoy the books that you WILL write.

Pastor Rob & Laura and our amazing Shoreline Church Family - Austin & Dallas, TX, the Kirk Franklin Team/Family, Ultimate Mastermind Crew, Jonathan Sprinkles, James Malinchak and all my friends and family... Wow & Thank YOU!

To every eye and heart that assisted in this project: Love and Change, Comfort Miller, Dr. Kathy Brooks, Santita Prather, Lexie Smith, Dale & Michal Dye, Colleen Matthews, Robin Pundzak, Nancy Lambertson, Travis Twomey & April Kearney... I see differently after walking and working with you.

To Rosalie Jerome: thank you for sharing your wisdom and experience, and inspiring me to "celebrate" my Sabbath and not just "do" it!

To my friends that have prayed me through this project: Our His Design team, Lara Izokaitis, Teresa Garcia, Adrian Lindsey, Sheri Irion, The Bevelle's and so many more.

To the brave women that have inspired this message within me and encouraged me by living a life worth emulating: Pat Lawson, Helen Hall, & Pastor Laura Koke.

To my other amazing mentors in life: Stephanie Ramirez, Coach Tom & Dorothy Reed, Lakita Wright, Amy Polus, & Lynette Lewis... U ROCK and look amazing doing your thang!

References

American Institute of Stress (AIS). (2010, April). Job stress. Retrieved from http://www.stress.org/job.htm

American Institute of Stress (AIS). (2010, August). Job stress: America's #1 health problem? Retrieved from http://www.stress.org/americas.htm

BLB. (2011, August 28). Blue Letter Bible. Retrieved from http://www.blueletterbible.org

Caplan, Lisa. (2010, January). Stress management. Retrieved from http://www.msba.org/departments/commpubl/publications/bar_bult/2010/january/lawyerassist.asp

Editor. (1997). New American Standard Bible. La Habra, CA: Foundation Publications, Inc.

Leaf, Caroline. (2009). Who Switched Off My Brain: Controlling Toxic Thoughts and Emotions. Nashville: Thomas Nelson Publishers.

Mandel, Michael. (2005, October 3). The real reasons you're working so hard… and what you can do about it. Bloomberg BusinessWeek. Retrieved from http://www.businessweek.com/magazine/cotent/05_40/b3953601.htm

Merriam-Webster Dictionary. (2011). Retrieved from http://www.merriam-webster.com

Oz, Mehmet. (2010, April 26). "Stress-Proof Your Life." Retrieved from http://www.doctoroz.com/walgreens-challenges/stress-proof-your-life

Webb, Brian T. (2011, August 10). Strong's Concordance. iPhone version 1.53.

Wikipedia. (2011, August 10). "Work Life Balance" Wikipedia: The Free Encyclopedia. Retrived from http://en.wikipedia.org/wiki/Work%E2%80%93life_balance

Life Balance Wheels

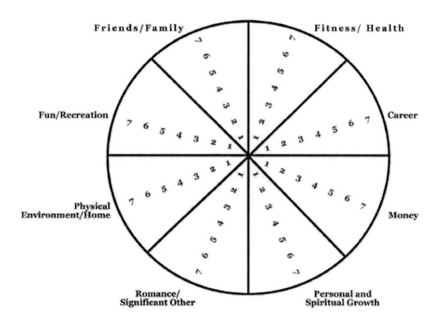

Additional life wheels from exercise in Chapter 1

Life Balance Wheels

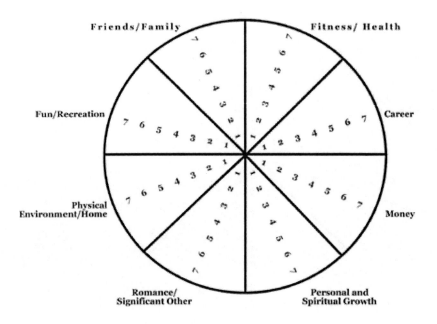

Additional life wheels from exercise in Chapter 1

"How do I make a difference?"
"What makes me unique?"

BLUEPRINT
CLARIFYING YOUR DESIGN

blū• prĭnt'(n). a workshop designed to bring greater clarity for men & women of all ages through truth, motivation, teaching and powerful exercises.

Benefits:

A full day of interactive coaching and training to *clarify...*

DID YOU KNOW:
Only 45% of Americans are satisfied with their work; this is the lowest level recorded in 22 years.

Only 51% find their jobs interesting.

64% of workers under the age of 25 say they are unhappy at work.

what motivates you
your purpose
(personal & professional)
what you were created to do
your legacy

To register or learn more
go to:

www.HisDesignForSuccess.com

Personal Life Coaching
also available

CPSIA information can be obtained at www.ICGtesting.com
Printed in the USA
LVOW081657180812

294928LV00001B/19/P